Acknowledgement of Land & of the Traditional Owners of this Land

I would like to acknowledge the Gadigal people of the Eora Nation, upon whose stolen land I stand on today.
I recognise that this land was never terra nullius — the land belonging to these peoples was never ceded, given up, bought or sold.
I would like to pay my respects to Aboriginal Elders past, present and emerging, and I extend this acknowledgement to all Aboriginal and Torres Strait Islander people.

This book is dedicated to all those people who feel that they don't fit in.

-"The Don"

Foreword

Vito Radice, "*The Don*", has written and published many short stories a talent I never knew he had, about his life, the era, the music and his adventures, including his poems with a "twist".

Poems for "*Misfits, Miscreants, Misanthropes, Mavericks, Losers & Malcontents*", a masterpiece of personal thoughts on , any subject , time and event, all scrambled into poetic verse with logical meaning.

What about, "*Poems for Restless Minds & Restless Hearts*", what a title. Don't we all go through this stage at least once in our life time. Here you will find poems on anything that will surely put you at ease. "*The Don's*" view and "spin" on things that will get you deep in thought & with a little "chuckle", at the same time.

I say, his book titles are "bizarre", his poems can be " bizarre", his choice of vocabulary "not mainstream " but then , in a world of perfection and Artificial Intelligence, his stories and " style" are HUMANISTIC.

I am grateful for having a good friend like Vito Radice "*The Don*".

You friend,
Jack Sciara
October, 2020

"The Don"
By Daniela Dali

Contents

1: I Just Had to Run Away
(Dovevo Solo Scappare)
2: Never Let Worlds Collide
(Non Lasciare Mai che i Mondi si Scontrino)
3: The Girl with the Most Beautiful Smile in the Whole World
(La Ragazza con il Sorriso Più Bello del Mondo)
4: The Act of a Desperate Lo♥er
(L'atto di un Amante Disperato)
5: Live in "The MOMENT"
(Vivi nil "Momento")
6: What If?
(Cosa Succede Se?)
7: LO♥E is a Bitch
(L'amore è una Cagna)
8: Season of the Witch
(Stagione della Strega)
9: True Lo♥e
(Vero Amore)
10: I Know You Want to Eat Me
(So che voi Mangiarmi)
11: Music is the Language of Lo♥e
(La Musica è il Linguaggio dell'Amore)
12: Life Rules
(Regole di Vita)
13: Rules of Lo♥e
(Regole d'Amore)
14: Passion
(Passione)
15: The Power of PASSION
(Il Potere della PASSIONE)
16: Immersion
(Immersione)
17: I Will Hurt You
(Io ti Farò del Male)

Contents

18: Woodstock
(Music & Art Fair)
(3 Days of Peace & Music)
19: Let Her Go
(Lasciala Andare)
20: Dance is the language of LIFE!
(La Danza è la Lingua della VITA!)
21: From your HE♥RT!
(Dal tuo Cuore!)
22: The River of Life
(Il Fiume della Vita)
23: Appreciate What You Have
(Apprezza Ciò Che Hai)
24: Better to Burn Out Than It Is to Rust
(Meglio Bruciare Che Arrugginire)
25: Look What They've Done
(Guarda Cosa Hanno Fatto)
26: Live Life
(Vivi la Vita)
27: Good Things Are Worth Waiting For
(Vale la Pena Aspettare Cose Buone)
28: This Is A Strange World We're Living In
(And These Are Strange Days)
(Questo è Uno Strano Mondo in cui Viviamo)
(e Questi Sono Giorni Strani)
29: Don't Trust People Who Don't Like...
(Non Fidarti delle Persone a Cui Non Piace ...)
30: I Won't Live Without Lo♥e!
(Non Vivrò Senza Amore!)
(Vincent Van Gogh)
31: I Have Learnt to Listen
(Ho Imparato ad Ascoltare)
32: If You Have an Itch, Scratch It!
(Se Hai Prurito, Grattalo!)

Contents

33: Puppet on a String
(Burattino Su Una Corda)
34: She Never Looks Back
(Non Si Guarda Mai Indietro)
35: Urban Growth
(Crescita Urbana)
36: Suffer Out Loud
(Soffri ad Alta Voce)
37: Wild He♥rt
(Cuore Selvaggio)
38: Lo♥e Shouldn't Be This Hard
(L'amore Non Dovrebbe Essere Così Difficile)
39: What Doesn't Kill you, Makes You Stronger!
(Ciò Che Non ti Uccide ti Rende Più Forte!)
40: Don't Be Tamed!
(Non Essere Domato!)
41: Green Out
(Verde Spento)
42: Dead He♥rt
(Cuore Morto)
43: Australia Street
(Via Australie)
44: Don't Let the Child in You Die
(Non Lasciare che il Bambino che è in te Muoia)
45: Independent Kat
(Gatto Indipendente)
46: Say Nothing, Do Nothing
(Non Dire Niente, Non Fare Niente)
47: A Conversation About God
(Una Conversazione su Dio)
48: Seeking Security
(Alla Ricerca di Sicurezza)
49: Sacred
(Sacre)
50: Idiot Man
(Uomo Idioto)

I Just Had to Run Away

(Dovevo Solo Scappare)

You looked so happy standing next to *"your man"*.
I was so Jealous.
I freaked out.
I just had to run away.

The situation was too heavy for me.
I just couldn't handle it.
Seeing you so happy leaning into *"your man"*.
I just had to run away.

My head went into a spin.
Everything was caving in on me.
I just had to get out.
Seeing you so happy cuddling up to *"your man"*.
I just had to run away.

I was transported to another time & place in my life.
To when I was 24 years young, 37 years ago.
I had fallen in Lo♥e with a beautiful Greek Goddess called Maria.
But she Lo♥ed someone else.
I just had to get out.
Seeing her so happy cuddling up to *"her man"*.
I just had to run away.

I was reliving it all over again.
It was *"Déjà vu"*.
The suffering was just too much.
I just had to get out.
Seeing her so happy canoodling up to *"her man"*.
I just had to run away.

The angst.
The tormented He♥rt.
The tortured Soul.
I felt it all again, seeing you so happy cuddling up to *"your man"*.
I just had to run away.

I know just have to accept it.
I know I can no longer deny *"reality"*.
She will Never Lo♥e me like she does *"her man"*.
Because I saw her so happy standing next to *"her man"*.
I just had to run away.

I know just have to accept it.
I know I can no longer deny *"reality"*.
She will NEVER Lo♥e me like she does *"her man"*.
Because I saw her so happy standing next to *"her man"*.
I just had to run away.

I couldn't breathe.
I was suffocating.
My World was collapsing in on me.
Seeing you so happy up next to *"your man"*.
I just had to run away.

That's how I wanted to make you feel.
That's how I wanted to see when you were with me.
But I saw it when you were with someone else.
I saw you so happy cuddling up to *"your man"*.
I just had to run away.

I just had to get out.
I just had to escape.
"Reality" was just too much to take at that moment.
Seeing you so happy standing next to *"your man"*.
I just had to run away.
All I can say is,
"Live long & prosper!"

I just had to run away.

"The Don"
06.10.2020

Never Let Worlds Collide

(Non Lasciare Mai che i Mondi si Scontrino)

Never let Worlds come close.
Never let Worlds interact.
Never let Worlds clash.
Never let Worlds collide.

Nothing good ever comes from it.
Nothing positive results.
Nothing comes out of it well.
Never let Worlds collide.

Destruction is the inevitable result.
Destruction of your Mind.
Destruction of your He♥rt.
Destruction of your Soul.
Destruction of your Being.
Never let Worlds collide.

My World went dark.
My World became cold.
My World was destroyed.
Never let Worlds collide.

Save yourself.
Save yourself if you can.
Save your World from destruction.
Never let Worlds collide.

It makes you feel numb.
It makes you feel empty.
It makes you feel lifeless.
Never let Worlds collide.

Avoid it at all costs.
Avoid to save your life.
Avoid it to save your Life.
Never let Worlds collide.

When Worlds collide, a cataclysmic explosion occurs.
When Worlds collide, destruction of the Being results.
When Worlds collide, you are annihilated.
Never let Worlds collide.
Never let Worlds collide.
Never let Worlds collide.
Whatever you do,
NEVER let Worlds collide.

"The Don"
05.10.2020

The Girl with the Most Beautiful Smile in the Whole World

(La Ragazza con il Sorriso Più Bello del Mondo)

She comes from Sierra Leone.
On the West Coast of Africa.
She works at Lillipad's in Glebe.
Usually on the weekends.
She is the barista there.
She makes the best coffee in town.
"Oka" will tell you that's because she had the best teacher ever.
Her name is Elizabeth.
She's the girl with the most beautiful smile in the whole world.

It stretches all across her face.
From one ear to the other.
It is like a shining light in the darkness.
Beaming radiant & bright.
It makes me so happy to see her face in the mornings.
Her name is Elizabeth.
She's the girl with the most beautiful smile in the whole world.

She is dark & mysterious.
Some might even say "enigmatic".
I Lo♥e her sense of humour.
She laughs at my poor attempts to be funny.
She must think I'm an "idiot".
But I don't care.
I look forward to the weekends just to see her working there.
Her name is Elizabeth.
She's the girl with the most beautiful smile in the whole world.

I try to engage her in conversation.
I try to impress her with my knowledge.
I try to make her laugh.
Then I remember that she is working.
This is not the time or the place for such repartee.
She has to be professional & focus on her tasks,
Of making the best coffee in ol' Sydney town.
Her name is Elizabeth.
She's the girl with the most beautiful smile in the whole world.

I would like to get to know her better.
I would like to hear her story.
I would like to find out how she is here.
I would like to know about her life.
I would like to her plans for the future.
I would like to know what she's about.
Maybe I will, one day.
Her name is Elizabeth.
She's the girl with the most beautiful smile in the whole world.

If you ever want to meet her.
If you ever want to say hello.
If you ever want to experience her smile & beauty.
If you ever have the time.
Come on down to The Lillipad Café in Glebe.
There you'll meet "Oka" & the gang.
There you meet Elizabeth.
She's the girl with the most beautiful smile in the whole world.

"The Don"
05.10.2020

The Act of a Desperate Lo♥er

(L'atto di un Amante Disperato)

It happened on a Sunday night.
The *"Incident"*.
What *"Incident"*?
It wasn't an *"Incident"* really!

The *"Situation"*.
What *"Situation"*?
It wasn't a *"Situation"* really!

I just had a *"Melt down"*.
That's what I had!
A *"Melt down"*.
Simple as that.

I met her there.
Her boyfriend was there too.
I went to find her.
And I had a *"Melt down"*.

She asked me to meet him.
I told her I didn't want to.
She said *"Please, for me"*.
"It's a social situation".
I reluctantly agreed.
I followed her.
She introduced me.
We shook hands & greeted each cordially.

He had what I perceived, a smirk on his face.
I saw her standing beside him.
I then proceeded to have my very own private *"Melt down"*.
I spiralled out of control & left.
Exit stage left, literally!

My body went into palpitations.
I went into *"Psychic shock"*.
My mind went wild.
I couldn't control it anymore.
I still have reverberations now.
Days later.
Like the aftershocks from an earthquake.
I can still feel them vibrating down my arms.

Logic flies out the window.
Self-control is just a wonderful dream.
Replaced by emotional chaos.
Life becomes a *"dreamlike state of mind"*.
One in which *"Reality"* & *"Super-Reality"* merge.
A *"numb-like"* existence.
Like to be in *"The Twilight Zone"*.

In my mind it now has become a *"Lo♥e"* test.
A test to see if she Lo♥es me.
I still have butterflies in my stomach.
Have I lost her?
The last thing she texted was, *"I will call you when I can 😳😳"*.
I've taken this to mean, *"Don't call me! I'll call you!"*
"Leave me the fuck alone!".
So, I won't contact her anymore.
Only time will tell.
If she does, then I will know that..........

"The Don"
06.10.2020

Live in "The MOMENT"
(Vivi nil "Momento")

See in "The MOMENT!"
Breathe in "The MOMENT!"
Eat in "The MOMENT!"
Walk in "The MOMENT!"
Sit in "The MOMENT!"
Work in "The MOMENT!"
Laugh in "The MOMENT!"
Talk in "The MOMENT!"
Think in "The MOMENT!"
Feel in "The MOMENT!"
Lo♥e in "The MOMENT!"
Live in "The MOMENT!"
Die in "The MOMENT!"
Be in "The MOMENT!"
Exist in "The MOMENT!"

"The Don"
08.10.2020

What If?

(Cosa Succede Se?)

What if I'd been younger?
What if I'd been taller?
What if I'd been thinner?
What if I'd been fatter?
What if I'd had more hair?
What if I'd had a beard?
What if I'd had been smarter?
What if I'd had been dumber?
What if I'd had been more "Arty Farty"?
What if I'd had been attentive?
What if I'd had been kinder?
What if I'd listened more?
What if I'd bought her flowers?
What if I'd bought her a puppy?
What if I'd bought her chocolates?
What if I'd taken her to fancy restaurants?
What if I'd pretended not to like her?
What if I'd played "hard to get"?
What if I'd been nastier?
What if I'd been richer?
What if I'd been poorer?
What if I'd been sexier?
What if I'd been spiritual?
What if I'd been powerful?
What if I'd been weak?
What if I'd had tattoos?
What if I'd had a pony tail?
What if I'd had a "Man Bun"?
What if I'd played guitar for you?
What if I'd sung for you?
What if I'd had only one leg?

What if I'd ....?

Would that have made any difference?

"The Don"
09.10.2020

LO♥E is a Bitch

(L'amore è una Cagna)

LO♥E bites.
LO♥E stings.
LO♥E hurts.
LO♥E attacks.
LO♥E cheats.
LO♥E lies.
LO♥E fights.
LO♥E has not morality.
LO♥E does not know "Right" or Wrong".
LO♥E does not know "Good" or "Bad".
LO♥E takes no prisoners.
LO♥E respects no boundaries.
LO♥E has no end.
LO♥E walks its own path.
LO♥E follows no master.
LO♥E does what it likes.
LO♥E is FREEDOM.
LO♥E is not defined by Time or Space.
LO♥E is not confined by Time or Space.
LO♥E has no limits.
LO♥E controls ALL.
LO♥E dictates its own terms.
LO♥E is a "Black Hole".
LO♥E is the Sun.
LO♥E is emptiness!
LO♥E is all encompassing.
LO♥E is all consuming.
LO♥E will use you.
LO♥E will abuse you.
LO♥E will spit you out!
LO♥E will destroy you.
LO♥E will fulfill you.
LO♥E will complete you.
LO♥E is like nothing else.
LO♥E is a battlefield.
LO♥E is a FUCKER
LO♥E is a BITCH!

"The Don"
11.10.2020

Season of the Witch
(Stagione della Strega)

Things not working out?
Troubles coming your way?
Storms gathering over your head?
Bad weather predicted tonight?
It must be The Season of the Witch!

Do you hear footsteps behind you?
Unlucky.... in LO♥E ... again?
Unrequited LO♥E playing its old hand?
She walked out on you for another man?
It must be The Season of the Witch!

A good time gone bad?
A good world gone bad?
You got the blues over some woman?
Rejection reared its ugly head, again?
It must be The Season of the Witch!

You feel you've played this game before?
You feel you been dealt a bad hand?
You feel you've been here before?
You feel like the jilted man?
It must be The Season of the Witch!

Unlucky in LO♥E, once again?
You're thinking will you ever get this right?
Did you feel rushed?
Did you need more time!
Don't feel so bad, it must be The Season of the Witch!

Did you sing & play guitar for her?
Did you serenade her with your favourite song?
What was it again, I must've forgotten?
Was it "All Along the Watchtower", a Bob Dylan song?
It's ok, it must be The Season of the Witch!

Did you try to impress her with your wit & your wisdom?
Did you make her laugh with funny stories?
Did you get your best shot?
Did you give your ALL?
Don't worry, it must be The Season of the Witch!

How often can you keep doing this?
How much more of this can you take?
How old are you, it must've slipped my mind?
When are you gonna get off this train?
Because the Season of the Witch will NEVER end!

"The Don"
12.10.2020

True Love

(Vero Amore)

What is "true Love"?
What does that mean?
Is ALL Love but not "true"?
Is there such a thing as "fake" Love?
Surely, that cannot be Love?
If it is "fake"!

Is that like vegan bacon?
Vegan cheese?
Vegan eggs?
Vegan pork?
Vegan chicken?
Something like the real thing but not?

Is Love just Love?
Otherwise, it's not Love?
It's something similar to Love but not the real thing.
An approximation.
An almost but not quite.
So "fake" Love is like "Vegan" Love?
The Love you have when you don't want the real thing?

It's a funny conundrum we find ourselves in.
This thing called "True" Love.
Maybe we'll sort it out one day?
Or maybe not?
Although it's pretty clear in my mind.
Either it's Love or not.

Pretence is not Love.
"Pretend" Love!
"Fake" Love!
Is not Love!

"The Don"
13.10.2020

I Know You Want to Eat Me
(So che vuoi Mangiarmi)

I know you want to hold me.
I know you want to hug me.
I know you want to kiss me
I know you want to kiss me deeply.
I know you want to take off my clothes.
I know you want to see my naked body.
I know you want to stroke me.
I know you want to caress me.
I know you want to run your hands down my body.
I know you want to sleep with me.
I know you want to finger me.
I know you want to lick me.
I know you want to fuck me.
I know you want to make Lo♥e to me.
I know you want to eat me.

I know!

I know!

I know!

Don, I know!

"The Don"
13.10.2020

Music is the Language of Lo♥e
(La musica è il Linguaggio dell'Amore)

What language do you use to make LO♥E?
Is it folk?
Is it the Blues?
Is it Jazz?
Is it classical?
Is it The Tango?
Is it Flamenco?
Is it Gospel?
Is it Tribal?
Is it chanting?
Is it the Mambo?
Is it the Samba?
Is it bluegrass?
Is it psycho rockabilly?
Is it Rock'n'Roll?
Is it Pop?
Is it Gregorian Chants?
Is it Punk?
Is is Psychedelic?
Is it Tibetan?
Is is Middle Eastern?
Is it Brasileiro?

Music is in my VEINS!
I live & breathe music!
I think in music!
I write with music!
My life is music!
I am music!
My soul is music.
My thoughts are music.
My dreams are music
My He♥rt is music.
My Lo♥e is music.

We can make LO♥E by sending each other music we LO♥E!
The music will make LO♥E for us!

"The Don"
13.10.2020

Life Rules

(Regole di Vita)

What I do & have done:
Chase someone.
Begged someone to stay.
Don't know my own worth.
Didn't save space for people who really mattered.
Didn't accept what cannot be changed.
Pursued what wasn't for me.
Did Lo♥e myself.
Didn't have faith in myself.
Didn't believe in myself.

What I should do:
Don't chase anyone.
Don't beg anyone to stay.
Know your worth.
Save space for people who matter.
Accept what cannot be changed.
Leave what isn't for you.
Lo♥e yourself.
Have faith in yourself.
Believe in yourself.

"The Don"
14.10.2020

Rules of Love

(Regole d'Amore)

Love conquers.
Love destroys.
Love manifests.
Love suffers.
Love flares.
Love grows.
Love explodes.
Love surrenders.
Love hurts.
Love fades.
Love shines.
Love sinks.
Love stinks.
Love fucks.
Love sucks.
Love torments.
Love excites.
Love ignites.
Love rules.
Love feeds.
Love sacrifices.
Love tortures.
Love incites.
Love shouts.
Love screams.
Love yells.
Love freezes.
Love procrastinates.
Love withers.
Love kills.
Love DIES.

There are no rules of Love.
Love does whatever it wants.
Love is its own master.
Love cannot be controlled.

"The Don"
14.10.2020

Passion

(Passione)

A Life without Passion is FUTILE.
A Life without Passion is FUTILITY.
A Life without Passion is EMPTINESS.
A Life without Passion is LONELINESS.
A Life without Passion is PASSIONLESS.
A Life without Passion is SOULLESS.
A Life without Passion is HEARTLESS.
A Life without Passion is THOUGHTLESS.
A Life without Passion is CARELESS.
A Life without Passion is MEANINGLESS.
A Life without Passion is SADNESS.
A Life without Passion is WASTED.
A Life without Passion is SHAMEFUL.
A Life without Passion is CRAZINESS.
A Life without Passion is USELESS.
A Life without Passion is HOPELESSNESS.
A Life without Passion is FUCKED.
A Life without Passion is HEARTBREAKING.
A Life without Passion is FORLORN.
A Life without Passion is PATHETIC.
A Life without Passion is EMPTY.
A Life without Passion is DEATH

A Life without Passion is a Life without MUSIC.
A Life without Passion is a Life WASTED.
A Life without Passion is a Life not LIVED.

Don't waste your Life by living it without PASSION.
Live your Life with PASSION.

"The Dev"
14.10.2020

The Power of PASSION
(Il Potere della PASSIONE)

Passion can move MOUNTAINS.
Passion can take you to the STARS.
Passion can create a MASTERPIECE.
Passion can make you CRY.
Passion can write a SYMPHONY.
Passion can dance you to the end of LO♥E.
Passion can make you explode with DESIRE.
Passion can drive you to MADNESS.
Passion can set your HE♥RT on FIRE.
Passion can burn your SOUL.
Passion can turn back TIME.
Passion can set you FREE.
Passion can imprison you in TORMENT.
Passion can light up The DARKNESS.
Passion can shine like The SUN.

Passion can make you sing like PAVAROTTI.
Passion can make strum like a GUITAR.
Passion can make you play like a VIOLIN.
Passion can make you become IMMORTAL.
Passion can break through to the "OTHER SIDE".
Passion can make you paint like VAN GOGH.
Passion can make you see like LEONARDO Da VINCI.
Passion can make you here like BEETHOVEN.
Passion can make you sing like JANIS JOPLIN.
Passion can make you think like EINSTEIN.
Passion can make you feel like LEONARD COHEN.
Passion can make you breathe like a NEW BORN BABE.
Passion can make you die on your own SWORD.
Passion can make you live like you've NEVER LIVED BEFORE.
Passion can make you feel like you've LIVED A THOUSAND LIVES.

This is the Power of PASSION.

"The Don"
15.10.2020

Immersion
(Immersione)

Life is about submersion.
Life is about conversion.
Life is about subversion.
Life is about immersion.

Don't just float about.
Don't just skim on the surface.
Don't just lay around.
Don't just dip you toes in.

Jump in.
Dive in.
Plunge in.
Fall in.

Completely become consumed.
Completely become subsumed.
Completely become engulfed.
Completely become immersed.

Let it fill your lungs.
Let if fill your brain.
Let it fill you He♥rt.
Let it fill your Soul.

Breathe it.
Think it.
Dream it.
Lo♥e it.
Live it.
Die it!

"The Don"
15.10.2020

I Will Hurt You

(Io ti Farò del Male)

"Yes, I know!"
"You already have."
"But that's alright."
"One cannot live hoping they will never get hurt."
"That's LIFE!."
"We're gonna get hurt."
It's okay when you said, "I will hurt you!"

You can't stop living because you fear you might get hurt.
Accept it.
You WILL get HURT.
Accept it and move on.
"I will hurt you!", you said.

You cannot let fear rule your life.
You cannot let fear control you.
You cannot let fear decide your fate.
You cannot let fear choose your destiny.
Just because you said, "I will hurt you!"

You cannot predict The Future.
Who knows what will happen?
Are our actions set in stone?
Is The Future predetermined?
When you said, "I will hurt you!"

I say, "I'll take my chances!".
"I'm gonna get hurt anyway".
"If it's not you, it will be somebody else".
"I'll take my chances with you!"
I replied when you, "I will hurt you!"

"The Don"
16.10.2020

Woodstock

(Music & Art Fair)
(3 Days of Peace & Music)

It happened in up-state New York.
It was held on "Yazmar's Farm".
It was a celebration of music.
It went for 4 days.
From the 15th to the 18th of August, 1969.
It was so massive.
An extra day had to be added.

I was just 10 years young.
It was the end of the "Summer of LO♥E".
500,000 people went.
There was no violence.
There was just LO♥E.
Bob Dylan did not perform but he lived there.

The line-up was extraordinary.
Some musicians & bands you have heard of.
Others have faded into oblivion.
But they live on because they played,
Were a part of.
Were Immortalised.
In the greatest music event in human history.

32 musicians & bands in total played that long holiday weekend.
They were:
Day 1 - Friday, August 15th 1969:
- Richie Havens
- Sweetwater
- Bert Sommer
- Tim Hardin
- Ravi Shankar.
- Melanie.
- Arlo Guthrie
- Joan Baez

Day 2 - Saturday, August 16th 1969:
Quill
Country Joe McDonald
John B. Sebastian
Keef Hartley Band
Santana
Incredible String Band
Canned Heat
Grateful Dead
Leslie West & Mountain
Creedence Clearwater Revival
Janis Joplin
Sly & The Family Stone
The Who
Jefferson Airplane

Day 3 - Sunday, August 17th 1969
Joe Cocker
Country Joe & The Fish
Ten Years After
The Band
Johnny Winter
Blood Sweat & Tears
Crosby, Stills, Nash & Young

Day 4 - Monday, August 18th 1969:
Paul Butterfield Blues Band
Sha Na Na
Jimi Hendrix

It was a moment in time.
It changed history.
It defined a generation.
"The Woodstock Generation".
They would forever be linked.
And remembered because of Woodstock.
The festival of LO♥E, Art & above all MUSIC.

"We are stardust
We are golden
And we've got to get ourselves
Back to the garden.

Then can I walk beside you
I have come here to lose the smog
And I feel to be a cog in something turning
Well maybe it is just the time of year
Or maybe it's the time of man
I don't know who I am
But you know life is for learning.

We are stardust
We are golden
And we've got to get ourselves
Back to the garden.

By the time we got to Woodstock
We were half a million strong
And everywhere there was song and celebration
And I dreamed I saw the bombers
Riding shotgun in the sky
And they were turning into butterflies
Above our nation.

We are stardust
Billion year old carbon
We are golden
Caught in the devil's bargain
And we've got to get ourselves
Back to the garden."

Songwriter: Joni Mitchell

"The Don"
17.10.2020

Let Her Go

(Lasciala Andare)

The only way to win her is.
To let her go.
The only way to want her to stay is.
To let her go.
The only way to want her to need you is.
To let her go.
The only way to want her to pursue you is.
To let her go.
The only way to want her to seek you is.
To let her go.
The only way to want her to dream about you is.
To let her go.
The only way to want her to scream for you is.
To let her go.
The only way to want her to move for you is.
To let her go.
The only way to want her to want you is.
To let her go.
The only way to want her to Desire you is.
To let her go.
The only way to want her to hold you is.
To let her go.
The only way to want her to hug you is.
To let her go.
The only way to want her to kiss you is.
To let her go.
The only way to want her to sleep with you is.
To let her go.
The only way to want her to have sex with you is.
To let her go.
The only way to want her to fuck you is.
To let her go.
The only way to want her to LO❤E you is….

To let her go.

To let her go.

To let her go.

To let her go.

"The Don"
17.10.2020

Dance is the language of LIFE!

(La Danza è la Lingua della VITA!)

Feel the rhythm.
Feel the pulse.
Feel the energy.
Feel the music.

Move your feet.
Move your arms.
Move your legs.
Move your body.

Let yourself go.
Let yourself disappear.
Let yourself feel.
Let yourself see.

Become "One" with your music.
Become "One" with your He♥rt.
Become "One" with your Soul.
Become "One" with your Being.

Become "One" with the Universe.
Become "One" with the Cosmos.
Become "One" with the "Spiritual World".
Become "One" with the INFINITE.

You no longer EXIST.
You no longer SUFFER.
You no longer FEAR.
You no longer DIE.

You have broken the chains that bind you.
You have broken the bonds that hold you down.
You have broken the forces that control you.
You have broken the shackles that imprison you.

Now you are ENERGY.
Now you are LIGHT.
Now you are IMMORTAL.
Now you are FREE.

If "Music" is the language of LO♥E?
"Dance" is the language of LIFE!

"Dance me to your beauty with a burning violin
Dance me through the panic till I'm gathered safely in
Lift me like an olive branch and be my homeward dove
Dance me to the end of love
Dance me to the end of love.

Oh, let me see your beauty when the witnesses are gone
Let me feel you moving like they do in Babylon
Show me slowly what I only know the limits of
Dance me to the end of love
Dance me to the end of love.

Dance me to the wedding now, dance me on and on
Dance me very tenderly and dance me very long
We're both of us beneath our love, we're both of us above
Dance me to the end of love
Dance me to the end of love.

Dance me to the children who are asking to be born
Dance me through the curtains that our kisses have outworn
Raise a tent of shelter now, though every thread is torn
Dance me to the end of love.

Dance me to your beauty with a burning violin
Dance me through the panic till I'm gathered safely in
Touch me with your naked hand or touch me with your glove
Dance me to the end of love
Dance me to the end of love
Dance me to the end of love."

Songwriter: Leonard Cohen

"The Don"
17.10.2020

From your HE♥RT!
(Dal tuo Cuore!)

"SING from your HE♥RT!"
"DANCE from your HE♥RT!"
"MOVE from your HE♥RT!"
"SEE from your HE♥RT!"
"THINK from your HE♥RT!"
"SPEAK from your HE♥RT!"
"FEEL from your HE♥RT!"
"FUCK from your HE♥RT!"
"LO♥E from your HE♥RT!"
"LIVE from your HE♥RT!"
"BE from your HE♥RT!"
"DIE from your HE♥RT!"

"The Don"
18.10.2020

The River of Life

(Il Fiume della Vita)

Go down to the River.
The River of Life.
Going down to the River.
Me, myself & I.
Going down to the River.
The River of Life.
Going down to the River.
Down to the River to die.
Going down to the River.
The River of Life.
Down at the River.
The River of Life.
Down at the River.
Drink from the River of Life.
Down at the River.
The River of Life.
Down at the River.
Swim in the River of Life.
Down at the River.
The River of Life.
Take it, take it from the River of Life.
The River of Life.
Take it.
From the River of Life.
Come back, come back from the River of Life.
The River of Life.
Come back, back from the River of Life.
Come back from the River of Life.
Back from the River of Life.
Down at the River.
The River of Life.
Down at the River.
The River of Life.
I'm back, yes, I'm back.
From the River of Life.

"The Don"
19.10.2020

Appreciate What You Have
(Apprezza Ciò Che Hai)

Appreciate "*The Moment*".
Appreciate your *friends*.
Appreciate your *situation*.
Appreciate your *experiences*.
Appreciate your *feelings*.
Appreciate your "*World*".
Appreciate your *LO*❤*ES*.
Appreciate your *environment*.
Appreciate your *Planet*.
Appreciate your *Life*.

Appreciate all the people that come into your life.
Appreciate the "good" & the "bad".
Appreciate that you are healthy.
Appreciate what you have.
Appreciate & be thankful.
Appreciate the kindness of others.
Appreciate the beauty in others.
Appreciate that you're alive.
Appreciate LIFE.
Appreciate what you have.
Appreciate!
Appreciate!
Appreciate!
Appreciate!

"The Don"
20.10.2020

Better to Burn Out Than It Is to Rust
(Meglio Bruciare Che Arrugginire)

Wanna live a long time?
Wanna have a long life?
Wanna live "la dolce vita"?
Wanna live a "good life"?
Because it's better to burn out than it is to rust.

Don't waste your life away.
Don't become a vegetable.
Don't become a zombie.
Don't become a "Living Dead"!
Don't become a "Walking Dead"!

Live your life to the MAX.
Live your life to the FULLEST.
Live your life to the LIMIT.
Live your life to the MOSTEST.
Live your life to the The END.

Laugh till The End.
Dance till The End.
Sing till The End.
Drink till The End.
Make music till The End.
Be creative till The End.
Fuck till The End.
Get STONED till The End.
Make LO♥E till The End.

Drink till The End.
Make music till The End.
Be creative till The End.
Fuck till The End.
Get STONED till The End.
Make LO♥E till The End.

Never stop being SEXY.
Never stop being a CHILD.
Never stop GROW UP.
Never stop being YOUNG.
Never stop PARTYING.

Live your life till you DROP.
Burn the candle at BOTH ENDS.
Don't leave any juice in the TANK.
Don't stop RAGING.
Never lose your INNOCENCE.
Never grow OLD.

Play HARD.
Party HARD.
Rage HARD.
Live HARD.
Lo♥e HARD.

Old age ain't PRETTY.

Set your life on FIRE.
Because it's better to burn out than it is to RUST.

"The Don"
20.10.2020

Look What They've Done
(Guarda Cosa Hanno Fatto)

Look what they done to my brain.
Look what they done to my mind.
Look what they done to my He♥rt.
Look what they done to my Soul.
Look what they done to my Life.
Look what they done to my Being.
Look what they done to my Thoughts.
Look what they done to my Friends.
Look what they done to my Children.
Look what they done to my People.
Look what they done to my Ideas.
Look what they done to my Principles.
Look what they done to my Integrity.
Look what they done to my Hopes.
Look what they done to my Dreams.
Look what they done to my Future.
Look what they done to my World.
Look what they done to my Planet.
Look what they done to my Dignity.
Look what they done to my Humanity.
Look what they done.

"The Don"
22.10.2020

Live Life

(Vivi la Vita)

Live Life like there's no tomorrow.
Live Life like it's your last day.
Live Life like it's the end of the World.
Live Life like it's the end of days.
Live Life like it's the final moments.
Live Life like it's the final countdown.
Live Life like it's Midnight.
Live Life like it's the end of Time.
Live Life like it's your final curtain.
Live Life like it's your final Show.
Live Life like it's all "Over Red Rover".
Live Life like it's your final Call.
Live Life like it's the final roll of the Dice.
Live Life like it's the "Hand of Death" is on your shoulder.
Live Life like it's "Beelzebub" calling.
Live Life like it's the "Grim Reaper" behind you.
Live Life like it's Death come calling.

Live Life FAST.
Live Life HARD.
Live Life.
Live Life.

"The Don"
21.10.2020

Good Things Are Worth Waiting For

(Vale la Pena Aspettare Cose Buone)

Good things are worth looking for.
Good things are worth searching for.
Good things are worth protesting for.
Good things are worth marching for.
Good things are worth voting for.
Good things are worth thinking for.
Good things are worth praying for.
Good things are worth LO♥ING for.
Good things are worth struggling for.
Good things are worth fighting for.
Good things are worth dying for.
Good things are worth LIVING for.
Good things are worth WAITING for.

"The Don"
22.10.2020

This Is A Strange World We're Living In
(And These Are Strange Days)
(Questo è Uno Strano Mondo in cui Viviamo)
(e Questi Sono Giorni Strani)

Rising temperatures.
Floods.
Plagues.
Droughts.
Bushfires.
Pandemics.
This is a strange World We're Living In.

Extinctions of animal species.
Global Warming.
Massive Wildfires.
Enormous cyclones.
Polar ice caps melting.
Heat wave conditions across the planet.
This is a strange World We're Living In.
These are strange days indeed.

Massive amounts of corporate frauds.
Cities in "Lockdown" for months on end.
Global virus pandemic.
2 million people dead.
Sea temperature is rising.
Fish are dying.
Whales are committing suicide en mass!
This is a strange World We're Living In.
These are strange days indeed.

The "Me Too" movement is demanding changes.
The "Black Lives Matter" movement is demanding action.
There are riots in the cities.
Social unrest is everywhere.
People are rebelling.
The smell of "Revolution" is in the air.
Politicians running scared.
"Fake News" is making the news.
This is a strange World We're Living In.
These are strange days indeed.

Where does the answer lie?
What will be the solution?
Will we be able to sort out this mess?
What will be the outcome?
Will we be able to cut through all this confusion?
Where are we heading to?
Will this be our last stand?
Will "The End" be coming soon?
Are we doomed for extinction?
Or is there a light in this "Darkness"?
Are these our "Dark Ages"?
This is a strange World We're Living In.
These are strange days indeed.

Desperate times call for desperate measures.
Can we save our planet?
Can we save ourselves?
Can we save Humanity from extinction?
"Is the glass half full or half empty?"
Which side of the fence are you on?
Or are you sitting on the fence?
Time is running out.
No more time to muck about.
This is a strange World We're Living In.
These are strange days indeed.

"The Don"
23.10.2020

Don't Trust People Who Don't Like...

(Non Fidarti delle Persone a Cui Non Piace ...)

Don't trust people who don't drink.
Don't trust people who don't smoke "dope".
Don't trust people who don't like partying.
Don't trust people who don't like dancing.
Don't trust people who don't like singing.
Don't trust people who don't like pizza.
Don't trust people who don't like pasta.
Don't trust people who don't like beer.
Don't trust people who don't like "The Blues".
Don't trust people who don't like Django Reinhart.
Don't trust people who don't like sex.
Don't trust people who don't like fucking.
Don't trust people who don't like the environment.
Don't trust people who don't like people.
Don't trust people who don't like "Fucking Bitches".
Don't trust people who don't like LO♥E.
Don't trust people who don't like "The Don".

Don't trust people who don't like...

"Inspiration from "The Fucking Bitch".

"The Don"
24.10.2020

I Won't Live Without Lo♥e!
(Non Vivrò Senza Amore!)
(Vincent Van Gogh)

You had passion.
You had LO♥E in your He♥rt.
You suffered so much.
You saw beauty everywhere.
You looked at the world with different eyes.
You were not like all the rest.

You saw colours so intensely.
You put your emotions onto the canvas.
You applied the paint so thickly.
It jumps off the painting.
& hits you in your face.
Your reds are so red.
Your yellows are do yellow.
You captured your reality.
You put it on the canvas.
You left it for us to see.

I see you.
I feel you.
I hear you.
You suffered so.
I suffer with you.
But yet, all you saw was beauty.

You saw beauty in everyday things.
You saw beauty everywhere.
Yet you suffered so.
No one understood you.
No one saw your suffering.
You died alone.
You will never die.
Your paintings won't let you.

But I am with you now.
I see your world.
I see what you saw.
Your world was full of beauty.
Yet you were full of suffering.
It seems that only through suffering can one truly see the beauty in things.

"I put my heart & soul into my work."
-"Vincent"

"The only time I feel I'm alive is when I'm painting."
-"Vincent"

"Great things are done by a series of small things brought together."
-"Vincent"

"Only when I fall do I get up again."
-"Vincent"

"I would rather die of passion than of boredom."
-"Vincent"

"Someday Death will take us to another star."
-"Vincent"

"LO♥E is something eternal, some things may change but not the essence."
-"Vincent"

"The way to know life is to love many things."
-"Vincent"

"I will NOT live without LO♥E."
-"Vincent"

"Starry, starry night
Paint your palette blue and grey
Look out on a summer's day
With eyes that know the darkness in my soul
Shadows on the hills
Sketch the trees and the daffodils
Catch the breeze and the winter chills
In colours on the snowy linen land.

Now I understand
What you tried to say to me
And how you suffered for your sanity
And how you tried to set them free
They would not listen, they did not know how
Perhaps they'll listen now."

"Starry, starry night
Flaming flowers that brightly blaze
Swirling clouds in violet haze
Reflect in Vincent's eyes of china blue
Colours changing hue
Morning fields of amber grain
Weathered faces lined in pain
Are soothed beneath the artist's loving hand.

Now I understand
What you tried to say to me
And how you suffered for your sanity
And how you tried to set them free
They would not listen, they did not know how
Perhaps they'll listen now
For they could not love you
But still your love was true
And when no hope was left in sight
On that starry, starry night
You took your life, as lovers often do
But I could have told you, Vincent
This world was never meant for one
As beautiful as you.

Starry, starry night
Portraits hung in empty halls
Frameless heads on nameless walls
With eyes that watch the world and can't forget
Like the strangers that you've met
The ragged men in the ragged clothes
The silver thorn, a bloody rose
Lie crushed and broken on the virgin snow

Now I think I know
What you tried to say to me
And how you suffered for your sanity
And how you tried to set them free
They would not listen, they're not listening still
Perhaps they never will."

"Vincent (Starry, Starry Night) by Don McLean"

"The Don"
25.10.2020

I Have Learnt to Listen

(Ho Imparato ad Ascoltare)

I have learnt to be quiet.
I have learnt to keep my mouth shut.
I have learnt to not say a word.
I have learnt to not interrupt.
I have learnt to be thoughtful.

I've learnt to listen.
I'm practicing very hard.
I'm trying my BEST.
It doesn't come easy to me.
I always seem to have something to say.

I've learnt to listen.
It's still early days.
I'm still just getting the hang of it.
There's always something to say.
But I'm biting my tongue.
I'm pursuing my lips.

I've learnt to listen.
I don't have to say my opinions.
I don't have to try to say something witty.
I don't have to try to be a "SMART ARSE".
Just be quiet.
Just listen.
It's not that easy.

I've learnt to listen.
It's a lot harder than it seems.
It's a lot more difficult than it sounds.
Especially for me.
It might be easier for you.
But I'm trying very hard.
I'm focused on it.
I'm working solidly on it.

I've learnt to listen.
I'm learning to listen.
To listen.
To hear.
To see.
To feel.
To think.

I've learnt to listen.
I'm learning to listen.
I'm a "work in progress.
I will make mistakes.
But I've learnt to listen.
I'm learning to listen.

"The Don"
25.10.2020

If You Have an Itch, Scratch It!

(Se Hai Prurito, Grattalo!)

If you have a need, fulfil it.
If you have a want, satisfy it.
If you have a dream, realise it.
If you have a fetish, indulge it.
If you have a passion, pursue it.
If you have a Desire, feed it.
If you have an Ideal, live it.
If you have a goal, attain it.

If you wanna travel, go for it.
If you wanna create, create it.
If you wanna rebel, do it.
If you wanna fuck, pay for it.
If you wanna a life, live it.
If you wanna LO♥E, open up your HE♥RT to it.

If you have an itch, scratch it!

"The Don."
26.10.2020

Puppet on a String
(Burattino Su Una Corda)

Pull me this way.
Pull me that way.
Bend me here.
Bend me there.

Tell me what to do.
Tell me where to go.
Tell me what to say.
Tell me what to think.
Tell me what to feel.

You are in control of me.
You are in the driver's chair.
You are in the cockpit.
You are in my mind.

You are the boss of me.
You are my mind.
You have total control.
You pull the strings.

I have no thoughts of my own.
I have no mind of my own
I have no actions of my own.
I have no decisions of my own.
I have no feelings of my own.

I am just a " Puppet on a String".

"I wonder if one day that,
You'll say that, you care
If you say you love me madly,
I'll gladly, be there
Like a puppet on a string

Love is just like a merry-go-round
With all the fun of the fair
One day I'm feeling down on the ground
Then I'm up in the air
Are you leading me on?
Tomorrow will you be gone?

I wonder if one day that,
You'll say that, you care
If you love me madly,
I'll gladly, be there
Like a puppet on a string

I may win on the roundabout
Then I'll lose on the swings
In or out, there is never a doubt
Just who's pulling the strings
I'm all tied up to you
But where's it leading me to?

I wonder if one day that,
You'll say that, you care
If you say you love me madly,
I'll gladly, be there
Like a puppet on a string

I wonder if one day that,
You'll say that, you care
If you say you love me madly,
I'll gladly, be there
Like a puppet on a string

Like a puppet on a, string."

Performed by: Sandy Shaw
Writers: Bill Martin, Phil Coulter

"The Don"
16.09.2020

She Never Looks Back
(Non Si Guarda Mai Indietro)

She never turns her head.
She never turns around.
She walks straight ahead.
She never looks back.

Is this the way she lives her life?
Is this the way she thinks?
Is this how her mind works?
Because she never looks back.

Upwards & onwards.
Take no prisoners.
Have no regrets.
She never looks back.

She just keeps on moving on.
She's seems to be a "free" spirit.
She seems to be a "free" soul.
Because she never looks back.

But is she so "free" though?
Maybe, it's just a mask that she's wearing?
Maybe, she wants to be free like the rest of us.
Though, she never looks back.

I look at her as she walks away.
I watch her back expecting her to turn around.
I see her opening her door.
I keep watching, hoping.

She never looks back.

I walk away!

"The Don"
26.10.2020

Urban Growth

(Crescita Urbana)

Urban habitation.
Urban construction.
Urban destruction.
Urban jungle.
Urban monstrosity.
Urban decay.
Urban suicide.
Urban inhabitation.
Urban inebriation.
Urban concentration.
Urban fornication.
Urban excrement.
Urban overpopulation.
Urban annihilation.
Urban monopilisation.
Urban reclassification.
Urban exploitation.
Urban deforestation.
Urban garbage.
Urban poverty.
Urban property.
Urban reclamation.
Urban consolidation.
Urban repatriation.
Urban subjugation.
Urban litigation.
Urban suffering.
Urban loneliness.
Urban jungle.
Urban growth.

"The Don"
27.10.2020

Suffer Out Loud

(Soffri ad Alta Voce)

Do not suffer in silence.
Shout it out.
Let everyone know.
Release your rage.
Suffer out loud.

Tell the World.
Let it all out.
Do not keep it inside.
Do not suffer in silence.
Suffer out loud.

The World needs to know.
That you suffer deeply.
There is no point in suffering in silence.
Shout it to everyone.
Suffer out loud.

We are all suffering.
But do not keep it inside.
Everyone needs to know.
That there is no point suffering in silence.
Suffer out loud.

Shout it out from the rooftops.
Shout it as loud as you can.
Scream it until your lungs hurt.
Scream it until it becomes a siren.
Suffer out loud.

"I am suffering!"
"I am suffering!"
"I am suffering!"
"I am suffering!"

"The Don"
28.10.2020

Wild He♥rt
(Cuore Selvaggio)

Friendly He♥rt.
Hurtful He♥rt.
Sad He♥rt.
Sorrowful He♥rt.
Seductive He♥rt.
Sexy He♥rt.
Fuckable He♥rt.
Deep He♥rt.
Passionate He♥rt.
Soulful He♥rt.
Lo♥ing He♥rt.
Desirable He♥rt.
Crazy He♥rt.
Uncontrollable He♥rt.
Adventurous He♥rt.
Stormy He♥rt.
Flaming He♥rt.
Unfathomable He♥rt.
Mysterious He♥rt.
Enigmatic He♥rt.
Untamed He♥rt.
Heartful He♥rt.
Wild at He♥rt.

Wild He♥rt.

"The Don"
28.10.2020

Love Shouldn't Be This Hard
(L'amore Non Dovrebbe Essere Così Difficile)

Love shouldn't be this difficult.
Love shouldn't be this traumatic.
Love shouldn't be this dramatic.
Love shouldn't be this volatile.
Love shouldn't be this chaotic.
Love shouldn't be this sad.
Love shouldn't be this unhappy.
Love shouldn't be this cruel.
Love shouldn't be this problematic.
Love shouldn't be this destructive.
Love shouldn't be this sorrowful.
Love shouldn't be this angry.
Love shouldn't be this abusive.
Love shouldn't be this jealous.
Love shouldn't be this possessive.
Love shouldn't be this scary.
Love shouldn't be this awful.
Love shouldn't be this argumentative.
Love shouldn't be this polarising.
Love shouldn't be this belittling.
Love shouldn't be this brutal.
Love shouldn't be this hurtful.
Love shouldn't be this painful.
Love shouldn't be this hard.

"The Don"
28.10.2020

What Doesn't Kill you, Makes You Stronger!
(Ciò Che Non ti Uccide ti Rende Più Forte!)

That's what they say.
To get you through the hard times.
The painful times.
The suffering times.
What doesn't kill you will make you stronger.

I keep saying this to myself.
I repeat it over & over again.
I want to believe it so badly.
What doesn't kill you will make you stronger.

Tough times are hard to get through.
No matter what they happen to be.
It could be unrequited Lo❤e.
What doesn't kill you will make you stronger.

It could be the end of a relationship.
One in which things just work out.
You weren't being treated right.
What doesn't kill you will make you stronger.

You were not being respected.
You were thinking it was all your fault.
But you still LO❤ED them.
What doesn't kill you will make you stronger.

Maybe it's financial stress.
Your job is SHIT.
But you need money to survive.
What doesn't kill you will make you stronger.

So, you hang in there.
Hoping things will get better.
But they don't!
What doesn't kill you will make you stronger.

You have to make the tough decisions.
You have to take a move.
It's live or die by a thousand cuts.
What doesn't kill you will make you stronger.

You know there's a light at the end of the tunnel.
You know you're gonna get through this.
You just have to be tough & strong.
Because what doesn't kill you will make you stronger.

"The Don"
29.10.2020

Don't Be Tamed!

(Non Essere Domato!)

Don't be chained.
Don't be enchained.
Don't be imprisoned.
Don't be locked up.
Don't be domesticated.
Don't be domiciled.
Don't be tethered.
Don't be anchored.
Don't be entrenched.
Don't be swallowed.
Don't be procreative.
Don't be rooted.
Don't be stagnant.
Don't be placid.
Don't be flaccid.
Don't be limp.
Don't be "squared".
Don't be "boxed in".
Don't be "pigeonholed".
Don't be orthodox.
Don't be conventional.
Don't be "systemitised".
Don't be "entombed".
Don't be "buried alive".
Don't be "zombified".
Don't be "mummified".

Don't be neutered.
Don't be stupified.
Don't be stupid.
Don't be idiotic.
Don't be bought.
Don't be sold.
Don't be commodified.
Don't be objectified.
Don't be married.
Don't be confined.
Don't be defined.
Don't be boring.
Don't be determined.
Don't be prescribed.
Don't be abused.
Don't be attrified.
Don't be neutralised.
Don't be consumed.
Don't be subsumed.
Don't be Dehumanised.

Stay WILD!
Don't be TAMED!

Stay FERAL!
Don't be TAMED!

Stay REBELLIOUS!
Don't be TAMED!

Stay RADICAL!
Don't be TAMED!

"The Don"
29.10.2020

Green Out

(Verde Spento)

Black out.
White out.
Freak out.
Hole in head.
Blood everywhere.
Period pad on head.

Uber.
Emergency.
Do you know where you are?
What is your name?
What is your date of birth?
What day is today?
Follow the light with your eyes?
Remember these pictures.
Cup, keys, bird.
How did you do this?

Waiting.
Friend is tired & exhausted.
She is THE BEST.
Go home.
No need to wait.
Rest up.
I'll be ok.

What did you have?
I drank some beer.
I smoked some dope.
A lot?
Yep.
Do you know where you are?
What is your name?
What is your date of birth?
What day is today?
Follow the light with your eyes?
Do you remember those 3 pictures?
Cup, keys, bird.
Good.

Wheelchair ride.
Through corridors that are dead.
Empty rooms.
Where are all the patients?
CAT scan.
Shaved chest.
ECG test.
Tetanus injection.
Blood taken.
Do I have any?
I'm an ALIEN.

Do you know where you are?
What is your name?
What is your date of birth?
What day is today?
Follow the light with your eyes?
Do you remember those 3 pictures?
Cup, keys, bird.
Good.

You're all good to go.
No major damage done.
No stitches required.
Outside it's raining.
It's Saturday morning
31st of October.
Halloween.

It was a full moon.
It was gravity.
It was something more.
Of course it was!
What was that all about?
Events happen that can't be explained.
Life works in mysterious ways.

PEACE out.
LO♥E out.
NIGHT out.
MOON out.
GREEN out.

"Better to die from passion than of boredom".
-"Vincent Van Gogh.

"The Don"
01.11.2020

Dead He♥rt
(Cuore Morto)

They're walking.
They're talking.
But they're dead inside.
They have a Dead He♥rt.
They're He♥rt is Dead!

They're full of anger.
They're full of hated.
They have no LO♥E inside.
They have no LO♥E in their He♥rt.
Because they are Dead inside.
They have a Dead He♥rt.
They're He♥rt is Dead!

Don't let your He♥rt die.
Keep you He♥rt alive.
Keep LO♥E inside.
Keep LO♥E inside your He♥rt.
Otherwise, you'll be Dead inside.
You will have a Dead He♥rt.
You're He♥rt will be Dead!

"The Don"
01.11.2020

Australia Street

(Via Australie)

There are plenty of people to meet.
On Australia Street, Australia Street.
Some of them you can even greet.
On Australia Street, Australia Street.
There's a lot of fun to be had.
On Australia Street, Australia Street.
You can even be bad.
On Australia Street, Australia Street.
Everyone is happy.
On Australia Street, Australia Street.
No one is allowed to be sad.
On Australia Street, Australia Street.
Life's one big party.
On Australia Street, Australia Street.
Come along & see if you fit in.
On Australia Street, Australia Street.
You've gotta be cool though.
On Australia Street, Australia Street.
They don't allow just anyone in.
On Australia Street, Australia Street.
There are very strict entry requirements.
To enter Australia Street, Australia Street.
You'll have to pass a very rigorous test.
To enter Australia Street, Australia Street.
There is no "rif-raf".
In Australia Street, Australia Street.
Only the best kind of people
Live on Australia Street, Australia Street.
So, if you think you fit the bill.
To live on Australia Street, Australia Street.
Put you on the list.
For Australia Street, Australia Street.
You might have to wait a while.
To get into Australia Street, Australia Street.
It's a very long waiting list.
For Australia Street, Australia Street.
But it's definitely worth the wait.
For Australia Street, Australia Street.

I LO ❤ E.
Australia Street, Australia Street.
Come on over.
To Australia Street, Australia Street.

It's all happenin'
On Australia Street, Australia Street.
You're hearing what I'm sayin'
Australia Street, Australia Street.

"The Don"
01.11.2020

Don't Let the Child in You Die

(Non Lasciare che il Bambino che è in te Muoia)

Don't let it go.
Don't forget it.
Don't hide it.
Don't abandon it.
Don't neglect it.
Don't throw it away.
Don't deny it.
Don't smoother it.
Don't put it to sleep.
Don't run away from it.
Don't poison it.
Don't muzzle it.
Don't restrain it.
Don't imprison it.
Don't bottle it.
Don't punish it.
Don't control it.
Don't mute it.
Don't rebuke it.
Don't lose it.
Don't abuse it.
Don't annihilate it.
Don't obliterate it.
Don't mutilate it.
Don't confiscate it.
Don't fight it.
Don't expunge it.
Don't purge it.
Don't box it.
Don't stomp on it.
Don't kick it.
Don't starve it.
Don't destroy it.
Don't kill it.
Don't let it die.

Don't silence its voice.

Let it live FOREVER!

"The Don"
02.11.2020

Independent Kat
(Gatto Indipendente)

That Kat knows what it wants.
It doesn't need to be told.
It doesn't like to be ordered about.
It is its own boss.
It has a mind of its own.
It's an "Independent Kat".

It does whatever it wants.
Whenever it wants.
With whomever it wants.
It doesn't ask for permission.
Because it's an "Independent Kat".

It lives to its own rules.
It follows its own path.
It travels its own road.
It follows its own destiny.
It's an "Independent Kat".

It goes out when it likes.
Stays out all night sometimes.
It makes sure it has a wonderful life.
All the time.
Because it's an "Independent Kat".

It's a free thinker.
It's a free spirit.
It's a free soul.
It's a free He♥rt.
It's an "Independent Kat".

It'll come to you.
If it wants to.
It won't because it HAS to.
Oh nooooooooooooooooo!
Because it's an "Independent Kat".

If you call out to it.
It might listen.
Then, it might not.
It does just whatever it feels like.
That's an "Independent Kat".

It's a "Cool Kat".
That's for sure.
It's a "Top Kat"
Definitely.
It's an "Independent Kat".

It's a "Black Kat".
It owns the night.
It owns the darkness.
It can see where we can't.
Oh, to be an "Independent Kat".

"The Don"
02.11.2020

Say Nothing, Do Nothing
(Non Dire Niente, Non Fare Niente)

Sometimes you've just gotta,
Say nothing & do nothing.
That is all that's required.
That is your action.
That is your response.
That is your answer.
That is your behaviour.
To say nothing & do nothing.
And you've said it all.
You've done it all.
There's nothing else to be done.
Just say nothing & do nothing.

Let the night do your talking.
Let the night speak for you.
Let the Moon shine its light on you.
Let Moon work its magic.
It knows what to do.
It knows what to say.

Let the wind whisper its sweet songs.
Let it wrap its arms around you.
Let it do your talking.
Let it speak for you.
All you have to do is let go.
Give in to their power.
Accept their gifts.
Let them do their magic.
That's what they are meant to do.
Just say nothing & do nothing.

And the World will be good.

"The Don"
02.11.2020

A Conversation About God
(Una Conversazione su Dio)

Tell me about your relationship with God?
It's complicated.

Really?
Tell me why it complicated?
Because fundamentally I don't believe in the concept of an all-powerful being.

Really?
You mean you don't believe in God then?
I was brought up as a Catholic with all the rituals that go along with it.
Also, I am a scientist & so I see the world from a scientific point of view. S I have all these different aspects acting upon me.
It's not a question I spend too much time thinking about!
The concept of God is always there of course!
I refer to God a lot in my poetry!
So, as I said, it's complicated!
Put it this way, if God does exist, I think he/she/it would like me!

Wow!
You're have a good reason.
YEP!

Am surprised!
Yeah!
My relationship with God is improving day by day.
It's a process.
I talk to him like he's my best friend and I pray to him because he's my Father in heaven.
I don't judge people on their beliefs! I judge them on their ACTIONS!

Yeah.
What do you believe spiritually? (as far as what it takes to get to heaven)?
It's not what you say that's important to me, it's what you DO!
If you're an ARSEHOLE, believing in God is not going to make you a better person in my eyes!
I don't worry too much about what happens to me after I die! I'm interested in what I do whilst I'm living!
I put all my energy into living & living the best possible life I can!
This is what's tangible to me! What's real! The here & now! The rest will sort itself out!
I actually, believe that I'm a very spiritual person. But not in the orthodox, conventional way!
I follow my own path!

Hello, are you still there?

Have I bored you?

"Conversation with an "Insta" friend"

"The Don"
03.11.2020

Seeking Security
(Alla Ricerca di Sicurezza)

Life is finite.
LO♥E is unreliable
Relationships are volatile.
Friends come & go.
Friendships do last
Work is insecure.
Money is inadequate.
Parents are fucked.
Home life is a shit hole.
Youth doesn't last.
Beauty is subjective.
Talent is a matter of luck.
Health is a role of the dice.
Wealth is a "pipe" dream.
Travel, forget it.
Owning property, dream on.
Happiness is transitory.
Material possessions are an illusion.
World peace, don't make me laugh.
Equality for all, don't make me laugh.
Save the environment, get "real".
Honest politicians, you've got to be kidding!
Redistribution of wealth, hahahahaha!

Death is the ONLY certainty.

I'm only seeking shelter from the storm.
I'm only seeking a shoulder to rest my weary head upon.
I'm only seeking a body to hold onto.
I'm only seeking some LO♥E to keep warm.
I'm only seeking another soul to commune with.
I'm only seeking security before Death comes calling.

"The Don"
03.11.2020

Sacred

(Sacre)

Sacred Food.
Sacred Clothes.
Sacred Plants.
Sacred Animals.
Sacred Rivers.
Sacred Voices.
Sacred Words.
Sacred Music.
Sacred Language.
Sacred d Skies.
Sacred Stars.
Sacred Numbers.
Sacred Patterns.
Sacred Geometry.
Sacred Ceremonies.
Sacred Rituals.
Sacred Sites.
Sacred Knowledge.
Sacred Ways.
Sacred People.
Sacred Land
Sacred Country.
Sacred Lives.
Sacred Beauty.
Sacred Women.
Sacred Sex.
Sacred Soul.
Sacred Prayers.
Sacred LO♥E.
Sacred He♥rt.
Sacred Death.

"The Don"
05.11.2020

Idiot Man

(Uomo Idioto)

I'm a fool.
I'm a loser.
I'm a clutz.
I'm a heathen.
I'm a crazy.
I'm a mad.
I'm a sinner.
I'm a sadist.
I'm a masochist.
I'm a whinger.
I'm a whinner.
I'm a drunk.
I'm a misanthrope.
I'm a nihilist.
I'm a pessimist.
I'm an inept.
I'm a vacuous.
I'm a clown.
I'm a joke.
I'm a pathetic.
I'm a freak.
I'm a cretin.
I'm an ignoramus.
I'm an imbecile.
I'm an ALIEN.
I'm an IDIOT.

"The Don"
05.11.2020

Books written by "The Don"

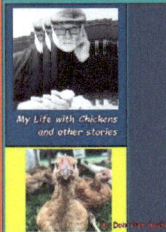
"My Life with Chickens & other stories: I Pity the Poor Immigrant"
Published:
10th September, 2019
Autobiography Book 1:
0 – 12 years old

"Poems for Misfits, Miscreants, Misanthropes, Mavericks, Losers & Malcontents!"
Published:
10th June, 2020
Book of Poems 1

"Poems for Troubled Minds & Trouble Hearts"
Published:
10th August, 2020
Book of Poems 2

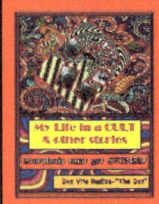
"My Life in a CULT & other stories: Everybody Must Get STONED!"
Published:
10th September, 2020
Autobiography Book 2:
15 – 30 years old

"Poems for Restless Minds & Restless Hearts"
Published:
10th October, 2020
Book of Poems 3

"Poems for Anarchists, Revolutionaries, Outlaws & Dissidents!"
Published:
10th November, 2020
Book of Poems 4

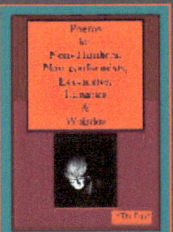
"Poems for Non-Thinkers & Eccentrics"
Published:
10th December, 2020
Book of Poems 5

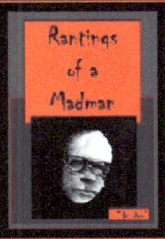
"The Rantings of a Madman"
Published:
10th January, 2021
Book of Poems 6

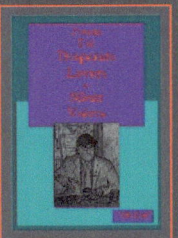
"Poems for Desperate Lovers & Silent Voices"
Published:
10th February, 2021
Book of Poems 7

"Poems for Tormented Minds & Tortured Souls"
Published:
10th March, 2021
Book of Poems 8

All available ONLY online

www.ingramcontent.com/pod-product-compliance
Lightning Source LLC
Chambersburg PA
CBHW041502010526
44107CB00049B/1622